PEACE

— and the —

SECOND COMING

Building the Kingdom
by Tearing Down Walls

LORENE DANIELS

PEACE AND THE SECOND COMING
BUILDING THE KINGDOM BY TEARING DOWN WALLS

iUniverse books may be ordered through booksellers or by contacting:

iUniverse
1663 Liberty Drive
Bloomington, IN 47403
www.iuniverse.com
1-800-Authors (1-800-288-4677)

ISBN: 978-1-5320-2380-4 (sc)
ISBN: 978-1-5320-2381-1 (e)

Library of Congress Control Number: 2017907298

Print information available on the last page.

iUniverse rev. date: 10/18/2017

DEDICATION

This Book is dedicated to my family, friends, and all who have given me their attention and listened to my ideas concerning biblical mysteries. It is my belief that when I reach out only one percent to God, God reaches out ninety-nine percent to me. That is because God loves me so much!

Lorene Daniels, Author

ACKNOWLEDGEMENTS

L oving gratitude is given to those who supported and encouraged me during the preparation for work in the ministry of pastoring and music. With honor I present this work in memory of those listed by an asterisk who have passed on and continue to cherish their memories and contributions:

Reverend Terri Earls
Barbara Washington
Reverend Jack Lane★
Dr. Joseph D. Cole★
Nyetta Barrett Royal★

CONTENTS

**Peace and the Second Coming: Building
the Kingdom by Tearing Down Walls**

In order to walk worthy of a calling, in my opinion, one must be first grounded in the religious experience. I agree with an idea espoused by A. J. Gita that once there is a religious experience, we can then operate with an understanding of that relationship. As a result, we are in a position to participate and have a relationship with the Divine. My inquiry into the mission of John the Beloved given by Jesus the Christ was primarily due to my asking existential questions in order to seek the truth. I asked the questions: Why would Jesus make such a reference to immortality for John the Beloved Disciple if it were not possible? What prompted the rumor within the community that John would not die? A theology of relationship places the point of connection on shared religious questions and experiences rather than belief or theology.

Even as a small child, I sought to test the existence of God through experience. My grandmother's theology was that of 'having an encounter with God'. This was a must and had to be experienced before her children and grandchildren could unite with the church before age twelve. One day she told me to stop jumping off the porch. When she was out of sight, I decided to continue jumping. When I did, I felt a hard slap on my right cheek that knocked me to the ground. It was so real that I never again disobeyed Big Mama, as she was lovingly called. I learned from that experience that God was so real that she could trade places with Him and supervise me even when she could not be seen.

When I reached adulthood, I had not considered that occurrence as a religious experience. While engaged in pastoral training, I was interviewed by an evaluation team for spiritual development. In my writing of the Life Script on spirituality which was required by the team, I included the slapping incident as my earliest experience with God. When the psychologist read it, she began to laugh out loud. She told me that at one time 'the slap' was used in a Catholic ritual for the Confirmation Sacrament with young children. She later gave me a copy of the ritual to confirm that, indeed, slapping had been used as a spiritual practice.

My spiritual experience from an early age was the impetus that sustained me in my thirty-seven year search on the mystery of the Beloved Disciple. I now live in amazement on the outcome of that search. I will forever be grateful to my spiritual mentor, the Reverend Jack Lane, who is now deceased. He was a faithful servant at the Fourth Missionary Baptist Church in Houston, Texas for many years. Over the years during my research, I often reflected on the spiritual wisdom he shared with me. I could see all the signs falling into place and directing me during my journey. I sincerely believe that there is much more to come.

One night I had a dream during our time together. I was wearing a sackcloth dress and brown sandals. An infant child was lying on my lap. Suddenly, the infant began to increase in size. At the same time, my body began to decrease. When I consulted Rev. Lane about the dream, he told me that as the Christ child increased in me, my personal self would decrease. I recognized it as a Scripture taken from John 3:30 where John the Baptist states, "He must increase, but I must decrease" referring to Jesus as the Messiah and himself as the friend of the Bridegroom, the one who was to come and prepare the way before him. As I pondered this sacred message, I was led to hide it in my heart.

CHAPTER 1

THE BEGINNING

In this book, I will try to connect the forty-fourth United States presidential administration of President Barack Obama and First Lady Michelle Obama with the world's third millennial occurrence, which is speculated to be between 2001 and 2033. Many have anticipated the awaited event to represent the second coming of Christ, which is spoken of in the Christian Bible. It reveals a time when Christ returns to earth and there is supreme peace. This book is also an extension of material taken from an inaugural sermon I preached on January 18, 2009, which will be discussed later in the text. It was titled *A Time of Peace: Building the Kingdom by Tearing Down Walls*.

This writing also connects the mystery of the "Beloved Disciple," John, a disciple of Jesus the Christ, who many believe did not die. According to John 21:19–23a, the disciple Peter asks the resurrected Jesus about the beloved disciple John and how he would die. Jesus said to him, "If it is my will that he remain until I come, what is that to you? Follow me!" So the rumor spread in the community that this disciple would not die.[1]

The good news for today's millennial generation is that there is a wave of righteousness and peace spreading across the land. The time

---

[1] John 21:19–23a NRSV

is now and long overdue for us to take our rightful position in the world as peacemakers. This applies to saint and sinner, the scholar and the illiterate, the young and the old. Those who have breath in their nostrils must inhale the aroma of the great shift taking place in world consciousness, which transforms hearts and minds from a state of illusion to light. This great shift that is widely spoken of in our time is a welcoming transition to the truth that sets us free. The wisdom and divine revelation of seers and prophets from more than two thousand years ago again speak to us through those who have ears to hear and choose to listen. One of those people spoke of the dream of peace for humanity as a rising star in American politics.

As I listened to the keynote address by a young black man during the 2004 Democratic National Convention, the birth of sacred peace seemed to be coming forth in the nation echoed then by the Illinois state senator, Barack Obama. He later became the forty-fourth president of the United States.

He spoke of oneness and the need to unite. He spoke of those walls that were preparing to divide us as a nation. They were identified as spin masters and negative ad peddlers who embrace the politics of anything goes. And he said to them, "There's not a liberal America and a conservative America - there's the United States of America. There's not a black America and white America and Latino America and Asian America; there's the United States of America." He went on to say, "I am my brother's keeper. I am my sister's keeper - that's what makes this country work. It's what allows us to pursue our individual dreams, yet still come together as a single American family: 'E Pluribus Unum.' Out of many, one."

During the time of his inauguration in 2009, I was serving as senior pastor of the Calvary United Methodist Church in Atlanta, Georgia. Church pastors had been asked to participate in a Sermons and Orations Project presented by the Library of Congress American Folklife Center in Washington, DC. We were asked to submit the sermons preached on January 18, 2009. These sermons would be proclaimed prior to the inauguration ceremony. The Folklife Center was working to catalog the sermons and orations received from all corners of the United States to commemorate the election of America's first African American president and have them available for researchers in the near future. A certificate was given to each one of us as a token of appreciation and gratitude for the submission.

The title of my submitted sermon, "A Time for Peace: Building the Kingdom by Tearing Down Walls," far exceeded my expectations considering that nine months into the former president's administration, he would be awarded the Nobel Peace Prize in 2009. My opening remarks to the congregation that Sunday morning began with, "Today there's a new sheriff in town, and he's here to keep the *peace*." And I believed *that* from the top of my head to the tip of my toes. My heart was telling me that he was indeed a peacemaker, a child of God. That day we dedicated our worship service to *the historic presidential inauguration that took place on* January 20, 2009. With grateful hearts, we praised God for his Word.

The sermon Scripture text came from Ephesians 2:13–14, 17–18:

> But now in Christ Jesus you who once were far off have been brought near by the blood of Christ. For he is our Peace; in his flesh he has made both groups into one and has broken down the dividing wall, that is, the hostility between us. … So he came and proclaimed peace to you who were far off and peace to those who were near; for through him both of us have access in one Spirit to the Father. (NRSV)

A Sermon by the Reverend Lorene Daniels, Senior Pastor, M.Div., M.Ed. of Calvary United Methodist Church, Atlanta, Georgia
Submitted to the American Folklife Center at the Library of Congress for the Inauguration 2009 Sermons and Orations Project

A Time for Peace: Building the Kingdom
by Tearing Down Walls
Preached Sunday, January 18, 2009

Scripture: Ephesians 2: 13-14; 17-18: (13) But now in Christ Jesus you who once were far off have been brought near by the blood of Christ. (14) For he is our peace; in his flesh he has made both groups into one and has broken down the dividing wall; that is, the hostility between us. (17) So he came and proclaimed peace to you who were far off and peace to those who were near; (18) for through him both of us have access in one Spirit to the Father.

In our text today the clarion call goes out to the Body of Christ which is the Church! The time is long over due for us to realize and take our rightful position in the church as "Peacemakers." As I reflected on the call for peace, I was remined of the Scripture in Matthew 5: 9. Jesus is speaking the Dream of God for humankind into those who have tried to keep the peace, those who chose the Bible instead of the bullet, the ones who chose passive resistance over physical confrontation. It is my interpretation that he speaks God's dream for the people using The Beatitudes. And as he speaks, he plants the seeds when he said, "Blessed are the peacemakers for they shall be called the children of God!"

Ephesians 2 is written to the church at Ephesus, and what is meant for them, still applies to the 21ˢᵗ century church today. In our passage the WALL was between the Jews and the Gentiles. It was a division created through racial hatred, cultural pride, religious tradition, and classism. Today we see walls of division in our neighborhoods. We build beautiful homes and then 'hold ourselves hostage' inside of them. We rarely go out of our way to make friends with neighbors, and consequently create enemies. Division and separation have existed between God's people since the beginning of time. But now it is a new day**. IT IS A TIME FOR PEACE. THE PEACE THAT TEARS DOWN WALLS AND ERECTS THE KINGDOM OF GOD IN THE HEARTS AND MINDS OF GOD'S CREATION.**

Jesus the Christ laid the foundation for such peace when he said, "On this rock I will build my church and the gates of hell shall not prevail against it." The children of God, the peacemakers, are the body of Christ and Jesus is the head. The body is designed to be in harmony with the head or it will not function properly. But as any good construction worker can tell you, 'before you can build, you must tear down!' Something has to go! In the olden days, people built fences for one reason, and one reason only: To keep the cows from getting out and going onto the neighbors' property. But we don't have cows anymore, at least not in the city. So, why are fences still around? The fence represents the wall of social division.

In the famous poem "Mending Wall" by Robert Frost, he tells about two neighbors who go through the same ritual each spring meeting at the fence to repair it. They have done this for many years. And it strikes the narrator in this poem to ask the question: Why is it that they have this wall in the first place? The line in the poem says:

And on the day we meet,
To walk the line,
And set the wall between us
Once again we keep the wall
Between us as we go

And from somewhere deep down in the soul of the narrator comes the realization: Something there is that doesn't love a wall. It's plainly spoken. There is something not quite right about this wall business. The neighbor goes on to explain to the other neighbor, "We don't need a wall. My apple trees will never get across and eat the cones under your pine trees." But the other neighbor only replies, "Good fences make good neighbors."

I ask the question this morning, "Do we need walls in the church?" Walls cause conflict, confusion and unending problems. They create conditions where the flesh is always in battle against the spirit.

The good news today is that there is a new wave of righteousness spreading across the land. As I listened to the keynote address by our president-elect, Barack Obama at the 2004 Democratic National Convention, I sensed a spirit of change coming forth in our nation. He spoke of oneness and the need to be united. He spoke of those walls that were preparing to divide us, the spin masters and negative peddlers who embraced the politics of anything goes. And he said to them, "There's not a liberal America and a conservative America, there's the United States of America. There's not a black America and white America and Latino America and Asian America. There's the United States of America." He went on to say, "I am my brother's keeper. I am my sister's keeper. That's what makes this country work. It's what allows us to pursue our individual dreams, yet still come together as a single American family. "E Pluribus Unum." Out of many, one."

Today there's a new sheriff in town, and he's here to keep the *Peace*. I believe in my heart that Mr. Obama is a peacemaker, a child of God. Today we dedicate our worship service to the historic presidential inauguration which will take place on January 20, 2009. President-elect Barack Obama serves as a symbol of the precious blood of Jesus Christ that connected the ones who were far off (Gentiles) to the ones who were near (Jews). Watch out World! There's a peacemaker in town that preaches and practices the gospel of peace. There is no longer a need to fight, no need or reason to look down on anyone, no need or reason to separate ourselves from one another. Our Scripture informs us that he who has made the two one, has destroyed the barrier, the wall of hostility; and through him the two have access to the one Spirit.

We are all united by the power of the Holy Spirit. The Holy Spirit wants to move in this world like it did on the Day of Pentecost in the early Christian church when all were on 'one accord.' Are we still the church of open arms, open hearts, and open minds? Or do we wall other people out? We need a revival in our churches that begins at the pulpit and reaches the door. Revival means to 'call back', or bring to life again or consciousness. As the old-timers use to say, 'take me back to the old landmark where I first found the Lord.' And if you don't have a landmark, then it's time to find one. We are asked in Ephesians 2, verse 11 to *remember*. When we go back and remember, we return to our senses and hear the words of Jesus saying, "The Holy Spirit will bring back to your remembrance all that I have told you." And in another place he says, "A new commandment I give unto you: Love one another as I have loved you!" But before we can love, we must tear down the walls that have been erected in our hearts. The work is not finished yet. It is still under construction. It is a work in progress. There are obstacles still being brought down. I'm reminded of the of the old gospel song:

> I'm working on the building
> It's a true foundation
> I'm holding up the bloodstained
> Banner for my Lord
>
> And as soon as I get through
> Working on the building
> I'm going up to Heaven
> To get my reward

I sincerely believe that president-elect Barack Obama has come at a time when humanity is awakening from the dream and illusion of separation. It is a time for peace. With our eyes wide open we can see that there is no place for walls. They just don't make sense! Just because it has always been that way, doesn't mean it has to stay. The truth about walls is that they are symbolic of human nature. But verse 14 tells us that Jesus Christ himself is our 'peace'. And when we take on Christ, the flesh no longer reigns but surrenders unto the spirit of the living Christ. This is not the peace we experience in the absence of war or hostility. It has roots in the Old Testament called *shalom*. It is a term which means salvation and life with God. It means wholeness, completeness, well-being and prosperity. In other words, *shalom is the way things should be.* Jesus' purpose was to create in himself one new person. And if anyone is in Christ, he or she is a new creature, making the many one.

Just look at the cross. It represents a restored relationship. It is both vertical and horizontal. The vertical represents the relationship between God and yourself and the horizontal represents the relationship between you and humankind. Jesus the Christ is our foundation, our chief cornerstone. In ancient days the cornerstone was the chief load-bearing stone. It determined how solid the building was going to be. That's why Jesus said, "Come unto me ye that labor and I will give you rest." And as we and president-elect Barack H. Obama stand on the rock, we will build the Kingdom of God by tearing down walls.

The invitation of Jesus Christ is offered to you today. It's an invitation that is always open. Have you had the dividing wall between you and God removed? Have you committed your life to Jesus Christ who so wants to destroy that wall for you? Do you want to turn from the sins of your past and make Jesus Lord of your life, be baptized and born again into this new life? Let me encourage you to do so today. The time is now. It is **A Time for Peace. Amen.**

CHAPTER 2

A TIME OF PEACE

With this peace comes a new meaning. It is far more than the absence of conflict or a state of calm and quiet. It is the peace of God that surpasses all understanding (Phil 4:7). The New Interpreter's Bible commentary (Eph 2: 13-14, 17-18) describes it as a total well-being which comes from God and is given to those who are in Christ and who share this attitude so that Christ's heart and mind become theirs.

According to the tradition of the early church era, the blood of Jesus Christ, shed at the Crucifixion, connected the ones who were "far off" (Gentiles) to the ones who were "near" (Jews). Today the hostility is between blacks and whites, liberals and conservatives, Republicans and Democrats, and immigrants and citizens. More than two thousand years have passed, and the work of Jesus Christ is still being carried out in our generation through the hands of peacemakers. It is being embodied by the leadership of wise and courageous men and women like President Barak Obama and First Lady Michelle Obama. The proclamation for peace continues through the vision and political efforts of President Obama. The Norwegian Nobel Committee recognized his work and awarded him the Nobel Peace Prize in 2009. They cited and recognized his extraordinary efforts to promote international diplomacy and cooperation between nations with a focus on having a world without nuclear weapons.

I foresee our present time of peace taking place in the early stages as characterized by the dissolution of hostility, separation, and division in our nation. These changes may appear violent and traumatic at first, as typified in the first coming of the Prince of Peace (the birth of Jesus), but they will be necessary for truth to be revealed. The Christ encountered persecution, rejection, and grand-scale misunderstandings. Strangely, these conditions existed among early Christian church communities as well. Humanity—and Christianity in particular—has been blindsided by directing attention too much on sin when the focus should have been on separation from God through disobedience.

Everyone, for some reason, wants the human error that occurred in the Garden of Eden to be caused by a villain called sin. However, studies by Professor Norman Cohn in his book *Cosmos, Chaos, and the World to Come: The Ancient Roots of Apocalyptic Faith*[2] reveals that the concept and origin of sin was not found once mentioned in the early Yahwist or Hebrew Scriptures but was introduced to the Jews during their exile in Maccabean times. This doctrine of dualism (good and evil) was later adopted into their writings. We also see where early conflicts between the apostolic church, led by the disciple Peter, and the Johannine community headed by the Beloved Disciple, John, were recorded in documents held by the church fathers. It is reflected in early church records and documents that there was a split between the two communities. Documentation can be found in the book *Peter and the Beloved Disciple: Figures for a Community in Crisis,* by Kevin

---

[2] Norman Chon, *Cosmos, Chaos, and the World to Come: The Ancient Roots of Apocalyptic Faith* (New Haven and London: Yale University Press, 1993).

Quast.[3] Unfortunately, details and references to the schisms are not explicitly given in our canonical Scriptures.

The word *canon* relates to those books of the Bible that early church authorities considered to be inspired by God. The first ecclesiastical church councils to form the cannon were held in North Africa at Hippo Regius in 393 AD and Carthage in 397 AD. Most scholars believe the term reflects the decisions of the councils to set up rules by which to live.

The Jews and conservative Christians hold to the authenticity of the thirty-nine books of the Old Testament as inspired, whereas the Evangelical Protestants view the twenty-seven books of the New Testament as inspired. Most Protestant denominations accept all sixty-six books as being inspired. Similarly, the Roman Catholics have a total of eighty books considering the inclusion of the Apocrypha (biblical writings that are not part of the canon of Scripture), which they regard as semicanonical. As we are sometimes overwhelmed by the many different beliefs and practices of the Christian faith, I find solace in John 21:25, which concludes that "There are also many other things which Jesus did; if everyone of them were written down, I suppose that the world itself could not contain the books that would be written."[4]

President Obama made a point to declare in his keynote address to the 2004 Democratic National Convention that, "I am my brother's and sister's keeper!" I believe that as a nation, we have a responsibility to watch over one another in love. As I reflect on a certain paradox of our modern society, there is increasing economic prosperity and high achievements in technology. But this state of affairs also seems to parallel a decline in civil behavior. We have been to the moon and back, but we still have trouble crossing the street to say hello to

---

[3] Kevin Quast, *Peter and the Beloved Disciple: Figures for a Community in Crisis* (Worcester: Billing and Sons Ltd, 1989).
[4] John 21:25 NRSV

a neighbor or picking up the phone to check on a friend. Hebrew 12: 14 tells us to "Pursue peace with everyone, and the holiness without which no one will see the Lord." The imperative in the text implies a directive that imposes an obligation or responsibility to the reader. We are to see that no one misses the grace of God. This is done by showing lost souls the way to God and life. See to it the that no root of bitterness springs up and cause trouble, and through it many become defiled and lost forever. This exhortation may just answer the question Cain asked God concerning Abel, "Am I my brother's keeper?" I believe that we have a responsibility to watch over one another in genuine love.

Wisdom is telling us that we have a responsibility to watch over one another in each other's human and spiritual growth. Showing concern and love is one of the identifying characteristics of a true disciple of Christ. In John 13: 35 Jesus said, "By this everyone will know that you are my disciples, if you have love for one another."

Believe it or not, and as simple as it may seem, this is a matter of life and death! Hebrews 10:26 tells us that when we knowingly continue and willfully persist in our disobedience to righteousness, after having received the knowledge of the truth, there no longer remains a sacrifice for wrong doings, but a fearful prospect of judgment. This is why we must take daily inventory of our own lives and warn our brothers and sisters of the seriousness of the matter. We must make it happen because a life is a terrible thing to waste!

When I look back over my life I thank God for people who watched over me and made sure I did not miss the grace of God in my life. My voice music professor, Dr. J.D. Cole, snatched me from under the bright lights of New York City and made sure I would not be devoured by the 'wolves in sheep clothing' in the music industry. He watched over me by recommending and securing me a music scholarship to college. Yes, He 'saw to it' that I didn't end up in the fast lane headed toward eternal destruction. He helped me make it happen. Not only that but when the storms of life were raging in my life, the billows were tossing high, my mother prayed for me. She saw to it that I didn't miss the grace of God. A song writer once said, "Somebody prayed for me, kept me on their mind, took the time to pray for me. I'm so glad she prayed for me."

CHAPTER 3

THE SEARCH FOR THE BELOVED DISCIPLE

From the beginning of my preparation for the calling into pastoral ministry in 1981, I have been doing personal research pertaining to the mystery of the Beloved Disciple John. My spiritual mentor at that time, the Reverend Jack Lane, had told me to read the four Gospels, Matthew, Mark, Luke, and John, three times each. The passage that captured my attention was from John 21:21–25 (NRSV). The disciple Peter was having a conversation with Jesus after his resurrection on the type of death he would die. He then asked Jesus about the type of death John would experience. In verse 22 Jesus states, "If it is my will that he remain until I come, what is that to you? Follow me!" This passage gave credence to the possibility that John the Beloved *could* remain on earth until he came again. It is assumed that he referred to the Second Coming. The passage goes on to say, that this saying went out to the community that this disciple would not die. We also suspect tension between Peter and John through the passage.

Of course, the question often crossed my mind of why Jesus would even want or need John, the disciple he loved, to remain on earth until he returned. Naturally, I came to feel that maybe it was because he was being rewarded or given some special honor. After all, he was often kept in anonymity by being referred to as "the

Beloved Disciple," which was also used in the Gospel. Baffled and intrigued by this passage, I shared my concerns with several ministers and theologians, hoping for insight on the issue, but I received no conclusive answers. What really baffled me was that no one had given it much attention, and no one seemed even curious about the matter. Surprisingly, I have found that there is a strong connection between the mission of John the Beloved and the new Millennium, which many believe is closely upon us.

A continuing school of thought on the mystery of John states that even though he was buried at Ephesus, he is not really dead but simply sleeps in the grave until the Second Coming of the Savior. But according to biblical tradition, it is suggested that John the beloved apostle never died but was to remain on earth until the Savior was to come again. In Luke 9:27 Jesus said, **"But truly I tell you, there are some standing here, who will not taste of death, before they see the kingdom of God."**

While this is not specific to John or Luke, Mark 9: 1 also reported this saying but added more substance to what Luke reported stating he said unto them, **"Truly I tell you, there are some standing here who will not taste death until they see that the kingdom of God has come with power."** Of course, the kingdom of God had already come in the person of Jesus Christ and he certainly *demonstrated* power. But he did not *come* in power. Quite the contrary. The coming of Jesus Christ was about as humble an entrance as one could imagine: Born in an animal shed, basically a barn or cave, surrounded by hay! However, Jesus' coming in power would not come until a later date. This is verified when the Lord spoke to his apostles of his second coming in Matthew 16: 27-28 saying, **"(27) For the Son of Man is to come with his angels in the glory of his Father, and then he will repay everyone for what has been done. (28) Truly I tell you, there are some standing**

here who will not taste death before they see the Son of Man coming in his kingdom."

The same problem exists in all three versions by different authors and that is the use of the word 'some' would imply there would be more than one who would not taste death. The other problem here is that all the apostle's deaths are accounted for except John. We find from Strong's Exhaustive Concordance of the Bible (Greek # 5100), the word for 'some' in all three of these instances is *tis*. Strictly speaking *tis* means 'some or person or object.' Therefore, we could easily say that 'some', in these instances, means 'some person' standing here shall not taste death until… The translators applied any number of different meanings to *tis* in various places, including, but not limited to 'somebody' and 'something'. Therefore, it is concluded, for better or for worse, that *tis* in these instances, is referring to 'some person' rather than 'some' in many. In addition, the (Greek # 3306) word for 'remain' is *meno*, meaning to stay in a given place, relation, or expectancy.

Nevertheless, regardless of what the authors meant, it was up to impetuous Peter to drag a little more information out of Jesus regarding this 'remaining' business. It seems obvious that something was different about John, or Peter wouldn't have bothered to ask what he did. And here we find the best evidence yet that it was John who would not taste death found in John 21: 20-24:

(20) Peter turned and saw the disciple who Jesus loved following them; he was the one who had reclined next to Jesus at the supper (John the beloved disciple) and had said, "Lord, who is it that is going to betray you?" (21) When Peter saw him, he said to Jesus, "Lord, what about him?" (22) Jesus said to him, "If it is my will that he remain until I come, what is that to you? Follow me!" (23) So the rumor spread in the community that this disciple would not die. Yet Jesus did not say to him that he would not die, but "If it is my will that he remain until I come, what is that to you:"

(24) This is the disciple who is testifying to these things and has written them, and we know that his testimony is true...

After three years of research, and spending many hours in the library, I finally had my breakthrough. As I was walking between rows of books, a paperback fell off the shelf and landed on my head. As I looked at it, I realized it was a book that contained information on people from the Far East who had experienced longevity. The title of the book was *In My Soul I Am Free* by author Brad Steiger.[5] It referred to John the Beloved, who was believed by the author to be still alive on earth today. It was so encouraging to finally find someone who seemed to hold an opinion on this mystery. I was not alone. From that point on, I was able to locate other authors, such as John Buchan, who wrote a book titled *Prester John*.[6] I could find only one copy left in print at the time, and I hurriedly put in the order. It was cited in the book that Prester John was linked to the mystery of the disciple John, who learned to transform himself into as many personalities as needed to perpetuate his existence and overcome death. He was said to have been living in a fabulous kingdom in the East during the Middle Ages. This new insight was like finding gold and made me more confident in my search for the truth.

---

[5] Brad Steiger, *In My Soul I Am Free* (Memlo Park: IWP, 1983).
[6] John Buchan, *Prester John* (New York: George H. Doran Company, 1910).

CHAPTER 4

THE NEW MINISTRY

After many years of carrying the burden of 'not knowing' surrounding the mystery of the beloved disciple, I finally came to realize that my search was being unconsciously carried out in my career and ministry endeavors. The recognition of this fact had a mystical effect upon me which made me realize God's omnipresence in this divine assignment. It encouraged me to continue the research. Years had passed with no new revelations on the matter, and I was kept busy with my seminary studies, which brought me to Atlanta, Georgia. It took me six years to complete my three-year course of study at the Interdenominational Theological Center. While working as a high school teacher, I would enroll every summer at ITC until my last year. After a while, I was able to get full early retirement, which allowed me to take the needed courses during my final year as required. I graduated, though worn and weary, with a master of divinity degree with honors in theology and church music. The Lord truly blessed my struggle. The week after graduation, in 2002, I became one of four associate pastors on staff at the Cascade United Methodist Church in Atlanta, Georgia. In retrospect, I now realize that my ministries in Atlanta were invisible threads that were connecting me to the root purpose of the secret mission of John the Beloved as given by Jesus: remaining on earth to protect the mystery of the very nature of Christ's return. More information will be given on the mystery later in the text.

My association with community organizations connected me with a group of Clergy Women in Atlanta. In 2007 I was honored to serve as host for an event they sponsored to bring former First Lady Michelle Obama to Atlanta during their first presidential campaign while I was the senior pastor of Calvary United Methodist Church in the city. It was one of the most electrifying encounters of my pastoral ministry. As Mrs. Obama approached the podium to speak at the event, the audience stood in honor of her presence. When I attempted to stand, my knees buckled, and I had to remain seated. As I sat in stillness, a quiet, small voice spoke to me, saying, "You are here to pray for her." From that day forward, the Calvary United Methodist Church and I, as senior pastor, kept the Obama family in prayer. During our VIP reception gathering for Mrs. Obama, I whispered in her ear that we would be in prayer for her family constantly. Today, I believe we were participating in a secret underground vigil that began over two thousand years ago under the guidance and leadership of the Beloved Disciple John.

During this time my pastoral ministry took on new meaning and focus. I felt there was an awakening occurring through the clarion call for unity in our nation and we were to be active in proclaiming it. Many church congregations in Atlanta opened their doors and homes to young people from all over the country who came to the city to work on the presidential campaign. They enthusiastically worked for the shaping and changing of a new America that would strive to become one nation under God, indivisible, with liberty and justice for all. This awakening gave testimony to the fact that 'the Lord our God is one'…and so are we! Our goal was to help tear down walls that divided us by learning to see ourselves as one through the mirror of relationships with others in our communities and families. We came to realize that we were one in the spirit in different forms, created this way to guarantee perfection in development of character through spiritual transformation into godly people. And in so doing, we learned that **'No thing fights against itself!'** There was a deliberate effort to cast aside our grievances and choose harmony through forgiveness. This change in our perspective brought about rivers of free flowing peace which was already latent within us.

One Sunday afternoon as I approached the steps to enter the church sanctuary during an evening worship service, I heard a voice that said, "Peace, my peace give I unto you." It was the familiar passage from a Scripture from John 14: verse 27. As I looked around to see who was talking to me, I noticed that no one was there talking to me. The crowd of people with me continued to walk pass me. I noticed that it was loud enough to be audibly heard all around me. It was then that I realized that the presence of Jesus was speaking to me. It was the first time that I felt Jesus *personally* communicating with me because of his words from Scripture. Normally I didn't give a personality to the Spirit when spoken to and attributed it to God only. At that time, I had no idea of the full revelation of what that statement meant.

It took a while for me to grasp the purpose of the message and how it was related to me, my life, and my ministry. At that time I was only aware of the accepted meaning of the 'experience' of peace with no notion of questioning a higher realm or spiritual level.

We normally live what we know and remain at that level of consciousness until further awakened. John 14 had always gotten my attention. I always wondered what he meant when he said, "I go to prepare a place for you" in verse 3 and *where* he was going. The accepted belief from my religious training and the given tradition was that he was going to his 'Father's house' which we called heaven. What I didn't understand was why he told his disciples that he would prepare a place for them. He also said that he would come again and take them to the place where he would be. There was no indication from verses 2-4 that this would be two thousand years in the future!

Traditionally this Scripture is most times read at funerals. It creates an atmosphere of comfort for the family of the deceased loved ones. It suggests that they are going to 'heaven' and being with the Father and the Son. It serves as a great passage for future hope. My question on this interpretation is why does Jesus have to 'go and prepare' a place? We normally assume that heaven is already prepared. The words 'Let not your heart be troubled' in verse 1 is also repeated in verse 27. Jesus says, "Peace I leave with you, my peace I give to you…Do not let your hearts be troubled and do not let them be afraid." These passages show a connection that is supported by a promise of *Peace,* and that *peace* is Jesus himself. He says, *"My Peace I give you."*

After researching the New Interpreter's Bible Commentary (NIB) on John 14:1-13, an interpretation was given which offered another perspective on the passage. First, the interpretation warns that it is critical that the words of Jesus 'to my father's house' not to be taken to mean the same as 'heaven'. It is noted that throughout John's Gospel, location is always being used as a symbol for relationship. For example, in John 1:18, a metaphor for Jesus' physical location (in the bosom of the Father) is used to express the loving closeness of Jesus' relationship to God the Father. To say that Jesus comes from heaven is saying that he is originated from God. It explains that to know where Jesus is from is to know his relationship with God. It is also noted that in John 8:35-36, there is a parable about 'residence' of the slave and the Son which clearly demonstrates that the use of location with relationship is not always about a physical location like heaven. The reference to there being mansions, dwelling places, or rooms takes on a different meaning in John's Gospel than in the one which appear in Jewish literature elsewhere in the Bible, and always refers to mutual communion between God and Jesus. The commentary also indicates that in 14:23 the use of the noun 'home', which also translates as 'dwelling place' in the Greek, means to love and live with Jesus and God in a relationship. It also allows for the joining of others in this relationship, this house.

Plainly spoken, this metaphor or use of speech imagery, is saying that Jesus' return to the father will make it possible for all God's children to join in the relationship that he shares. This is John's (the beloved disciple) vision of the kingdom of God and Jesus' concluding promise: "So that where I am, there you may be also." Once we recognize and appreciate the special relationship Jesus had with 'the disciple he loved', we will begin to understand the unique bond relationship and how he expressed himself in speech on a different level. This explanation also more fully gives additional evidence as to why Jesus would give such a command to John to 'remain' until the Second Coming.

CHAPTER 5

THE HIDDEN MYSTERIES REVEALED

A second focus on peace which requires more clarity is located again in John 14: 27a which says, "Peace I leave with you. My peace I give to you." It wasn't until I read the NIB interpretation that I gained a greater understanding of Jesus' message to me on the church steps and how it related to my calling and specific ministry purpose.

This was said to be the first occurrence of the word peace (*eirene*) in the fourth Gospel. Traditionally, the Old Testament *peace (salom)* is said to be a leave-taking address; however, in John, Jesus is not giving a farewell speech. As a point of reference, this chapter is usually referenced and known biblically as **The Farewell Discourse John 14:1-16; 33.** In this setting surrounding the hour of Jesus' death, the verb 'to leave' (*aphiemi*) takes on the meaning of a bequest. In verse 18 Jesus promises not to leave the disciples 'orphans', and he promises his *peace*, that is, they will not be alone because they will live in the *peace of Jesus* (see chapter 16:33).

The commentary scholars see Jesus' repetition of 14: 1 in verse 27d, "Do not let your hearts be troubled" as reinforcing the need for the disciples to be vigilant and not see 'peace' as a time to be passive or inactive. This seemingly is a call for them to find strength, to take courage in this new challenge. This strength is, in reality, being made available through Jesus' life (see v. 19), his love (vv. 21,23), and his joy (15:11; 16:22; 17:13). Very close attention should be given to verses 18-20 wherein there is a continuing presence seen by biblical scholars of Jesus' *return* when he promises not to 'leave them orphaned'. His primary promise to *return* occurs in Jesus' EASTER APPEARANCE. The reality of these verses are revealed in the stories found in chapters 20-21. The clue, in verse 19, speaks of the post-resurrection appearance when Jesus says, "In a little while the world will no longer see me, but you will see me; because I live, you also will live." The proclamation that Jesus' *resurrection life gives life to the believers* stands firm and substantiated by the disciples and others. The Easter morning resurrection was the ultimate demonstration that he truly is the 'resurrection and the life'.

It would not be too difficult to imagine the many sacred and secret revelations Jesus shared with *the disciple John, whom he loved*. Jesus demonstrated his confidence and total trust in the disciple when he placed Mary, his mother, in John's care at the foot of the cross. It is said that love is surely a many-splendored thing. Allow me to paraphrase using Scripture: "What no eye has seen, nor ear heard, nor human heart conceived, what God has prepared for those who love him—these things God has revealed to us through the Spirit; For the Spirit searches everything, even the depths of God" (1 Cor. 2:9–10 NRSV).

As my research and preoccupation with the mystery of John the Beloved continued, I was drawn to writings by James Twyman, the Peace Troubadour, who travels around the world singing songs and praying prayers of peace. He is the best-selling author of *The Secret of the Beloved Disciple* and *Emissary of Light: Vision of Peace*. His book *The Proposing Tree* made the *New York Times* bestsellers list. The personal experience of the author brought home for me the connections between peace and the Second Coming. It put the missing pieces to the puzzle in place concerning the mystery of John as far as I can discern. In preparation for his leadership of the group called the Emissaries of Light in Bosnia in 1995, Twyman was informed that the group was an underground sect, the Johannine community, headed by John the Beloved, who he learned did not die but headed and prepared the group to hold the "light" for humanity while peace was being restored to earth.[7]

According to author Craig R. Koester in his book *Symbolism in the Fourth Gospel: Meaning, Mystery, Community*,[8] Mary is said to be a representative figure of the church. He found it remarkable that Jesus' mother was placed in John's care. Peter had run off from the persecution of the Savior and denied him three times. John followed the Redeemer and became Mary's son. During the Crucifixion, Jesus spoke from the cross. John 19:26–27 states, "When Jesus saw his mother and the disciple he loved standing beside her, he said to his mother, 'Woman, here is your son.' Then he said to the disciple, 'Here is your mother.' And from that hour the disciple took her into his own home" (NRSV).

This surely could have resulted in the conflict between the two disciples Peter and John. Koester further states that the words Jesus spoke—"Behold, your son, and behold, your mother"—resembled to some extent the formulas used for rites of adoption in the ancient world when two people who are connected by their faith relationship with Jesus rather than by kinship ties are brought together to form the nucleus of a new community of faith. While Peter was the commissioned leader for the institutional church, John had been commanded by Jesus to lead the new Johannine community of faith. At this time, the remaining disciples and other followers had different preferences for leadership. It was then, according to church

---

[7] James F. Twyman, *Emissary of Light: A Vision of Peace* (New York: Warner Books Inc., 1998).

[8] Craig R. Koester, *Symbolism in the Fourth Gospel: Meaning, Mystery, Community* (Minneapolis: Fortress Press, 1995).

scholars and writings of church fathers, that the outer church under Peter's authority, (see Matt. 16:18–20 NRSV) given by Jesus, and the Johannine community, sometimes referred to as the inner church led by John, went their separate ways. It is suspected that the Johannine group eventually went underground out of fear of persecution and being destroyed by the outer church. Conflicts in the Christian churches of the past and today should not surprise or discourage us. It appears to be inherent in the human condition while we are on earth.

Similarly, the Fourth Gospel, traditionally known to be written by John the Evangelist, was not as easily accepted by the early church fathers as the synoptic Gospels, Matthew, Mark, and Luke. It was the last authorized gospel to be written, and there were some accusations by the church councils of heresy noted in the writing that seemed to be connected to the teachings of the Gnostics whose beliefs were based on a personal inner religious experience. After much debate and controversy, it was finally considered to be authentic and given a place in the biblical canonical Scriptures. As we consider the struggle of the early churches (headed by Peter and John) after Jesus' ascension, I am driven to connect that conflict with the secret mission of John: **To guard and protect the hidden identity of the Christ for the Second Coming.**

It seems that the church that was built on a rock (see Matt. 18:16–20 NRSV) is still under construction, and each generation and dispensation must contribute to the wholeness of the structure. All peacemakers must become architects, working and building in these walls of time. This sentiment is expressed in some of the lines of the poem "The Builders" by Henry Wadsworth Longfellow:

All are architects of Fate,
Working in these walls of Time;
Some with massive deeds and great
Some with ornaments of rhyme.
Nothing useless is, or low;

Each thing in its place is best;
And what seems but idle show,
Strengthens and supports the rest.

It was the words of the Master in John 21 that made the quantum leap into the future for me, saying to Peter that John just might "remain until I come." It would seem reasonable to believe that someone had to be put in place to hold up the blood-stained banner as a soldier of the cross. And we know that John had a good track record as someone who was reliable, trustworthy, and committed to the work of Jesus. Now we are the soldiers of the cross, the Savior's peacemakers who must become beacons of light, replacing all illusions of error with light, and accept our calling as the guardians of peace.

CHAPTER 6

THE SECOND COMING

Theologians, scholars, seminarians, and pastors all speculate on the different aspects of the Second Coming taken from the Bible prophecies and scriptural teachings of the Old and New Testaments with varying interpretations. We know there are several stages associated with end-time prophecies that have been traditionally accepted by the Christian church as cited in the book of Revelation. When Jesus was asked by his disciples, "Tell us, when will this be, and what will be the signs of your coming and of the end of the age?" (Matt. 24:36,42 NRSV), he replied, "But about that day and hour no one knows, neither the angels of heaven, nor the Son, but only the Father … Keep awake therefore, for you do not know on what day your Lord is coming." In 1 John 3:2 we see a message saying:

> Beloved, we are God's children now; what we will be
> has not yet been revealed. What we do know is this:
> when he is revealed, we will be like him. (NRSV)

An end-time event that speaks to a thousand-year period found in Revelation 20:1-6 (NRSV) is called by many the new Millennium, a time of peace when Satan is bound and locked up for a thousand years so he would not deceive the nations any more until the thousand years were ended. At this time, some seated on thrones are given the authority to judge. The souls of those who had been beheaded for their testimony of Jesus are brought back to life and reign with Christ for a thousand years. In face of obscure and varying theological interpretations on "eschatology" (teachings and predictions on the Second Coming) and seeming miscalculations by religious sects who clearly anticipated the Second Coming shortly after the ascension of Jesus, it would be wise to be ready and prepared at all times. Perhaps we may be asking the wrong questions. Instead of asking, "When will it occur?" or "What will be the signs?" we may need to ask, "*How* will the Second Coming Christ be revealed?"

The call now goes out to the body of Christ, which is the church, the inner sanctuary, where God inhabits the praise of his people. The time is long overdue for us to take our rightful position as peacemakers. As I reflected on the Lord's call for peace, I was reminded of the Scripture in Matthew 5:9 (NRSV). For me Jesus is speaking the dream of God for humankind into those who have tried to keep the peace, those who chose the truth of the Bible instead of the bullet, the ones who chose passive resistance over a physical confrontation. From my perspective, he speaks God's dream to the people by delivering the Beatitudes. And as he speaks, the seeds of compassion and peace are planted when he says, "Blessed are the Peacemakers for they shall be called the Children of God!"

Ephesians 2:13–14, 17–18 (NRSV, inaugural sermon text that gave birth to this book) was written to the church at Ephesus. Keep in mind that what was meant for them still applies and is essential for the twenty-first-century church today. The wall was between the Jews and the Gentiles. It was a division created through racial hatred, cultural pride, religious traditions, and classism. It was separation! Today we see walls of division in our neighborhoods. We build beautiful homes and then hold ourselves hostage inside of them. We rarely go out of our way to make friends with our neighbors and consequently create enemies.

One day I was reminded of this when I desperately tried to carry out two large bags of garbage to the trash bin in my subdivision. An elderly man was sitting on the side walk in a wheelchair. He looked lonely and a little sad. Regardless of my overload and my skepticism about approaching strange men, I felt a need to share with him by extending my usual 'hi' and 'bye' and maybe an inquiry on how his day was going. He gave me a big smile and started talking about his arthritis pain and the contributing weather which was hot and humid. After dumping the garbage, I made a point to come near him. I spent some time, exchanged pleasantries, and learned is name. He then told me that I was an unusual person in his broken English and Spanish accent. He added that most people in the neighborhood rarely spoke to each other. I felt his heart reaching out to me and I was deeply grateful for the opportunity to be a friend.

Division and separation have existed between God's people much too long. We are now at crossroads in our lives. We are in a place where we must make a decision on which path to take. We are in a time when peace, *permanent peace,* is being born into our world through peacemakers in our midst. It is the time for peace… the peace that tears down walls of separation and erects the Kingdom of God in the hearts, minds, and even the molecular structure of God's creations in this world. We come in contact with God's children of Light everyday without knowing it. Pay attention and be aware of miracles occurring in our everyday lives! Don't be afraid to look people in their eyes. Help them to be open to the miracle in you.

CHAPTER 7

SECRETS OF THE NEW WORLD

After reading *The Secret of the Beloved Disciple* by James Twyman, I was captivated by the story of his acquaintance with a student by the name of Maria. He met her during a march in Belgrade. To his surprise, she became more of a spiritual guide during his encounter with the Emissaries in Bosnia. He later learned that she was a physical manifestation of Mary, the mother of Jesus. She told him that she used a physical body to teach him a specific lesson and that when the lesson was finished, the body would be gone. I feel that the impact of this conversation between the two could be more clearly understood by using the direct quotes from the book. This took place in 1997 during Twyman's trip to Medjugorge:[9]

> "The Emissaries of Light have been praying for the enlightenment of humanity for two-thousand years, and yet when It came time to end their mission they came to you. Why?"

---

[9] James F. Twyman, *The Secret of the Beloved Disciple* (Scotland: Findhorn Press, 2004), 85-89.

"I never found out." I said to her. "I figured it was because I was there … available. I never read much more into it than that."

"But there is more," she said. "A great deal more. And you've already begun to remember. You've begun to understand who the Emissaries really are."

"You mean the 'Community of the Beloved Disciple,' don't you? So it is true. The Emissaries come from the lineage of St. John. When the church began persecuting the order they went underground and have remained there ever since. That means that John's role has been fulfilled. Jesus said that John would remain until he came again, or at least his community would. The fact that the Emissaries have disbanded must mean that he has returned. John himself is not here to witness it, but the community he started is."

"No, he meant what he said," Maria said to me. "John has remained, and is here right now."

"I don't understand," I said. "Do you mean reincarnation?"

"The idea you have of reincarnation is a fantasy," she said to me. "The truth is much simpler than you expect … and more complicated, depending upon how you look at it. John never left the earth, and neither did Jesus."

"Are you saying that they've been on earth for the last two thousand years? But how is that possible?"

"You believe that this realm is limited to the physical world you perceive," she said. "There are many other levels of reality you have yet to perceive, and they are just as real as this one. It is from these deeper levels that the essential work has taken place. It was to this realm that Jesus ascended after his resurrection, and it is there that he has remained, along with John and many others, waiting for the time of the great shift. You can consider them a group of overseers, kind of a board of directors."

"The Emissaries were the physical counterpart of this unique group, made up of beings who have achieved mastery on this level of existence, from every religion and spiritual path. There are other levels of reality beyond the one where John and Jesus work, what you might call the angelic realms. The Emissaries were like an anchor point that served as a physical link between all these etheric planes and the physical world."

"We've all been taught that Jesus ascended into Heaven," I said to her, "and I would expect St. John to be there as well. It sounds like you're saying that they were somewhere in-between, and that they will someday leave the realm and return to earth."

Maria smiled when I said these words, a loving smile, but the kind one gives a child when they don't understand. "You can call it Heaven if you want. In many ways it is very similar to your concept of Heaven. And yet there is so much more, many other levels that are so subtle you have no way of understanding them. The masters do not return from these levels physically, unless it's in a form like you're perceiving right now. I have assumed this body in order to teach you a particular lesson. When the lesson is over, the body is gone."

"What returns to the world is what you might call an 'energetic signature.' For example, the Christ is an experience, not a person. Please understand this because it is of vital importance – Jesus was certainly the Christ, but the Christ is not limited to your idea of who Jesus was. Jesus assumed that frame of reference, or that energetic signature, and therefore became the Savior of his age. The teacher you are waiting for, what you call the 'next teacher', will assume the same frame of reference as Jesus. It will be the same, and yet it will be different. It will be Jesus, but it will be more."

"I'm not sure if I understand," I said. "What about the Second Coming? Does Jesus ever come back to earth, or is it his soul that returns?"

"It is both, and it is neither," she said. "I am sorry that it doesn't make logical sense, but there's no way to understand it logically. Jesus, beyond his body and personality, has always been present on the etheric levels waiting to return to earth. This is the predestined time of awakening, the moment when 'The Christ' returns to *initiate* the New World. But it will not happen the way you think. In other words, don't expect a Jewish man with a beard to appear and save the world. And that brings us back to John and the society he founded."

"Before Jesus died on the cross he put me, his mother, in the care of John," she continued. "From that day on I was cared for by the apostle as well as the disciples that followed him. He was with me when I was assumed into the real world, and many years later he followed the same path. He did not die a physical death as is believed. He has continued as a living master to the community he founded, and most importantly has protected the greatest mystery of all –the very nature of Christ's return. You see there are actually two manifestations of the Christ energy. For the last two thousand years Jesus, in his identity as the masculine Christ, has personified that manifestation. The New World I spoke of is essentially a shifting of poles. The energy of the Christ, just as everything must, is about to find balance."

"I'm still not following this," I said to her frustrated. "Shrinat Devi said something similar—that there is another Christ … but what does this have to do with St. John?"

"For two thousand years John has cared for and protected what you're calling the 'next teacher'," she said. "He took her into his home and into his heart … and is now bringing her back to the world."

"But you said that you are not the one I've been waiting for," I said, "and yet you are the one he cared for. Doesn't that mean you're the 'next teacher'?"

"No, but the energy I carry is," she said to me. "Look past your idea of who you think I am, past this appearance or the way you were raised to believe in me. It is the feminine nature of God that I bring, the energy of compassion and peace. John's role was not only to protect that energy, but to give it back to the world. And that is what John is now doing— through you."

"Now, the Roman Catholic Church has always taught that the pope is the successor of St. Peter, the first pope. It also teaches that a sacred relationship is established each time a new pope takes office, and that the new leader acts 'as Peter'. This is the true meaning of papal infallibility. It has nothing to do with reincarnation, but everything to do with 'energetic signature.' The pope actually enters an energy field that was once occupied by the apostle himself. Whether or not the new pope accepts and activates that energy field is another question, but it is there nonetheless."

"The same has been true of the inner church as well," she said. "Since the ascension of John there has been hundreds of people who have stepped into the energy field he left behind, just as the pope steps into the energy field left by St. Peter. Each one of them has continued the sacred task of holding the 'feminine Christ' in their heart, guarding and loving that light until the time would come for it to be activated. They have acted 'as John,' and have carried out the mission given to John. When the church became so afraid of this lineage that it tried to have it destroyed, the most secret branch of the order went underground to preserve the mission. They have been known by many names, the Cathars, the Knights Templar, the Bogomils, and most recently as the Emissaries of Light. They have existed for two thousand years, and it has not come to an end, only shifted direction."

This revelation from Twyman almost took my breath away. Prior to this discovery, I felt I had come to the end of the journey on my search for the treasured revelation on the building of the kingdom of God. It was welcoming to find that I was indeed correct, and I experienced a sigh of relief after waiting so many years. I had carried a solid conviction on this mystery in my heart and had waited patiently for that moment. The book was not based on speculations but a first-had encounter by someone who had not even given much attention to the mystery. He is also known as the Peace Troubadour and has performed music at peace concerts in such countries as Iraq, Northern Ireland, Bosnia, Serbia, Kosovo, and Mexico, as well as at the United Nations in New York.

In the above conversation, the reference to the two manifestations of Christ as being the masculine and feminine energy fields align with today's scientific data concerning the "shifting of poles" in our universe. It also reminded me of the passage in Revelation 21:1–4 where John the Revelator saw the holy city, the new Jerusalem, coming down from heaven as a bride adorned for her husband. Could this symbolism possibly have something to do with the feminine and male polarity of God? In holy matrimony, it is said that the male and female become one. "It is done!" in verse 6 appears to indicate that something was completed, as if a balance had taken place. Perhaps this is a Scripture that could undergo further research.

Our new gospel of peace and love goes hand in hand with the new Millennium. It is to be lived, preached, and thus activated in the hearts of new believers and peacemakers. We must also understand that God's plan for the evolution of humankind manifests as a community of peace. It requires the personal acceptance and participation of those who make the decision to accept it. This peace of God surpasses all understanding and exceeds all powers. We should welcome this new beginning with open hearts and open minds.

CHAPTER 8

THE GIFT OF IMMORTALITY

The belief in and acceptance of John's immortality was not difficult for me. From early childhood, I enjoyed engaging in the otherworldly aspects of life in general. Anything I could not figure out I found myself creating through a colorful imagination. There was nothing that seemed impossible at that developmental stage of my life. This consideration surrounding John's "remaining" on earth appeared to be a spiritual phenomenon occurring in a natural scheme of true reality. It was even more evident that immortality on earth was possible after reading Mark 9:2–10. In this Scripture, Jesus shared a biblical encounter on the Mount of Transfiguration with Peter, James, and John as witnesses. It states:

> Six days later, Jesus took with him Peter and James and John, and led them up a high mountain apart, by themselves. And he was transfigured before them, and his clothes became dazzling white, such as no one on earth could bleach them. And there appeared to them Elijah with Moses, who were talking with Jesus. Then Peter said to Jesus, "Rabbi, it is good for us to be here; let us make three dwellings, one for you, one for Moses, and one for Elijah." He did not

know what to say, for they were terrified. Then a cloud overshadowed them, and from the cloud there came a voice, "This is my Son, the Beloved; listen to him!" Suddenly when they looked around, they saw no one with them anymore, but only Jesus. As they were coming down the mountain, he ordered them to tell no one about what they had seen, until after the Son of Man had risen from the dead. So they kept the matter to themselves, questioning what this rising from the dead could mean. (NRSV)

Elijah and Moses were two prophets from the Old Testament who were said to have never tasted death. Elijah was carried away (out of sight) on a chariot, and Moses's grave is said to have never been located. Also, a prophet named Enoch who was said to have walked with God did not taste death. It appears that humanity has just assumed that these men went to some other world or place. Several Scriptures clearly confirm (see Matt. 16:28, Mark 9:1, Luke 9:27, John 8:52) that there would be some person in the crowd who would not taste death until Jesus would be seen coming in his glory. Another Scripture that has always raised my curiosity is taken from Matthew 17:9–13, which states:

As they were coming down from the mountain, Jesus ordered them, "Tell no one about the vision until after the Son of Man has been raised from the dead." And the disciples asked him, "Why, then, do the scribes say that Elijah must come first?" He replied, "Elijah is indeed coming and will restore all things; but I tell you that Elijah has already come, and they did not recognize him but they did to him whatever they pleased. So also the Son of Man is about to suffer at their hands." Then the disciples understood that *he was speaking to them about John the Baptist.* (NRSV)

Scripture gives us living proof of God's plan for immortality through the lives and testimony of pioneers such as Enoch, Elijah, and Moses. Even Lazarus and Jesus Christ were raised up from death to life and resurrected.

When considering these biblical accounts, I am curious as to why the spiritual community has not examined this phenomenon and shed more light on the matter. It seems that humankind ignores that which they do not understand and is satisfied with leaving it in the realm of the mysterious. Some believe that Jesus spoke in hypothetical terms. However, having found no evidence to the contrary in his sayings, I believe that the Beloved Disciple continues to live with us today, the here and now, on an earthly plane.

Addressing this enigma and bringing it to light for consideration is most important to me. Secrecy was one of the conditions Jesus imposed on some of his disciples regarding hidden revelation knowledge. The book of Mark is laden with "don't tell" admonitions to the twelve. But in Luke 8:10, we find Jesus saying to his disciples, "To you it has been given to know the secrets of the kingdom of God; but to others I speak in parables so that looking they may not perceive, and listening they may not understand." (NRSV). Brothers and sisters, welcome to the kingdom of God!

According to "An Essay on the Scriptural Doctrine of Immortality" by author James Challis,[10] it is surprising that the word *immortality* obtained a place in the systems of philosophy. He further states that the authors must not have been accustomed to the idea of divine revelation. He feels that in the absence of such aid, the belief of immortality should not have been firmly held and probably

---

[10] James Challis, "An Essay on the Scriptural Doctrine of Immortality." http://Biblehub.Com, June 5, 1862. (Web) (14 Nov. 2014)

should have been disavowed. From thorough and intensive research, Challis reveals that biblical scholars recognize that the words *immortal* and *immortality* occur only in the Epistle of the Apostle Paul in the canonical Scriptures and consequently not until the subject of eternal life and immortality had been brought to light through the Gospels. However, these words are said to be met with more frequency in the apocryphal books of 2 Esdras, Wisdom of Solomon, and Ecclesiasticus (books not recognized for acceptance) than in the canonical Scriptures. This apparent silence of the Scriptures, especially in the Old Testament, on such an essential doctrine has generated much speculation among scholars.

As we look at the information in the Epistle of the Apostle Paul, we get a clear and inspired picture of divine revelation on the subject. First Corinthians 15:51–55 states:

> "Listen, I tell you a mystery! We will not all die, but we will all be changed, in a moment, in a twinkling of an eye, at the last trumpet. For the trumpet will sound, and the dead will be raised imperishable, and we will be changed. For this perishable body must put on imperishability, and this mortal body puts on immortality. When this perishable body puts on imperishability, and this mortal body puts on immortality, then the saying that is written will be fulfilled: "Death has been swallowed up in victory. Where O death is your victory? Where O death is your sting?" (NRSV)

It is often said that as in the natural, so in the spiritual world, assuming that the Creator executes divine purposes in alignment with specific laws. In respect to this rule, St. Paul in Romans 8:2 writes of the "law of sin and death." It reads:

> For the law of the Spirit in Jesus Christ has set you
> free from the law of sin and death. (NRSV)

This explains that sin and death are akin to each other. Death is ordained by an element that is incapable of being recalled and is considered to be "the wages of sin" (Rom. 6:23 NRSV). It does not contain within itself the power and wisdom of an almighty God that the sinful should live forever. And knowing this is so, it is also safe to say that immortality, being excused from death, is the consequence of freedom from sin, or we might call it perfection. This appears to make the case for immortality for humankind.

Earlier in the text I spoke on the emergence of the concept of sin, which came from the doctrine of dualism (good and evil). This doctrine was introduced to the Jews while in Maccabean exile by the Zoroastrians. Harold Bloom, in his *Omens of Millennium*,[11] concurs that the fundamental imaginings of the prophet Zoroaster are a separation of all reality into two forces, God and the devil. Prior to this time, there was no mention or evidence of such a concept in the Hebrew Bible or Yahwistic literature according to biblical scholars and research. The Jewish communities held to the conviction in their Shema prayer: "Hear O Israel: the Lord our God is one Lord!" (Deuteronomy 6:4 KJV). Please keep in mind while reading quotes from other biblical passages forthcoming that they do not reflect my earlier preferred concept used for sin when discussing it in this particular chapter.

It is believed that if sin is understood to be doing what is contrary to the will of God, as expressed by a command, then righteousness, being its opposite, will consist in acting according to his will. It is on this principle that St. Paul says, "Apart from the law sin is dead" (Rom. 8:8 NRSV), and in another place speaks of the "righteousness

---

[11] Harold Bloom, *Omens of Millennium: The Gnosis of Angels, Dreams, and Resurrection* (New York: Riverhead Books, 1996).

of the *law"* being fulfilled (Rom. 8:4 NRSV). Accordingly, when Adam was placed in the Garden of Eden, a command was expressly given for trial of his obedience. The narrative in Scripture of the circumstances under which sin was first committed is here deserving of special consideration on account of the instruction it conveys. It states that Eve, knowing that God had commanded Adam not to eat of the tree of the knowledge of good and evil, yet being deceived by the serpent and enticed by her own desires, "took of the fruit thereof, and did eat, and gave also to her husband with her, and he did eat" (Gen. 3:6 NRSV).

St. Paul further writes that "Adam was not deceived, but the woman being deceived was in the transgression" (1 Tim. 2:14 NRSV). However, both partook of the forbidden fruit, and by doing so, both presumably sinned alike against their Maker, the deed being construed as sinful, *not as considered by itself* but by reason of the antecedent (a preceding event) command, which made it an act of *disobedience*.

Some scholars have speculated that as soon as it was shown by the sin of Adam that the natural man was incapable of obedience to the will of God, a preordained dispensation was begun, whereby the natural man is converted into the spiritual man made fit for immortality. It is thought that this dispensation was introduced by a promise, the terms of which could be understood by Adam and Eve after they had learned that the spirit of evil (in whom is the "power of death') through disobedience brought death into the world. The promise was given in the words "He shall bruise thy head, and thou shall bruise his heel" (Genesis 3:15). Hebrew commentators have taken this passage in the sense that he ("the seed of the woman") shall bruise thee at the *ending*, and thou shalt bruise him at his *beginning*. The promise, accordingly signifies that the power of Satan would prevail at first, and for a time, even to putting to death the Son of God (Luke 22:53) but in the end that power would by the Son of God be overcome (Luke 10: 18). And since with the victory over the spirit of evil an end is put to evil itself, the promise is, in effect, that Adam and his race shall eventually be exempt from death and evil, and partake of a happy immortality.

It is said that as soon as it was shown by the sin of Adam that the natural man is incapable of obedience to the will of God, a promise was made whereby the natural man is converted into the spiritual man and made fit for immortality. An announcement given by God to the serpent, "He (the seed of the woman, Christ) shall bruise thee at the *ending* of the final unfoldment of creation and you shall bruise him at the *beginning*" was put in place. Jesus the Christ, the second Adam, put an end to evil itself which made the first Adam and his race exempt from death.

St. Paul states "But the spiritual is not first, but the physical (or natural), then the spiritual. Paul calls the first Adam a "living being" and the second Adam, Christ, a "life-giving spirit." Below is a chart which may be helpful in the understanding of the Adam-Christ typology.

The First Adam	**The Last Adam**
Living being	*Life-giving spirit*
The physical/natural	*The spiritual*
Made of earth	*From heaven*
Those who are of earth	*Those who are of heaven*

As for the natural creation of humankind and immortality after the grave, two remarkable sayings of our Lord is recorded in John's Gospel. He first says, "The hour is coming, and now is when the dead shall hear the voice of the Son of God; and they that hear shall live." (John 5:25) and then in vv. 28-29 of the same chapter he says, "The hour is coming in which all that are in their graves shall hear his voice, and shall come forth; they that have done good, unto resurrection of life; and they that have done evil, unto the resurrection of judgment" (kriseos). The first passage refers to a partial resurrection inasmuch as it makes mention of those only who shall hear the voice of the Son of God, and hearing shall live; whereas the other passage asserts that all who are in sepulchers shall hear his voice, and divides these into two classes: Those that have done good, who rise to live (the class just before mentioned), and those that have done evil, who rise to be judged. The assertion in vv. 28-29 is, accordingly, a revelation respecting the resurrection of all the dead, and is to be taken as comprehensive of the other. The class that will partake of "the resurrection of life" are the same as those of whom it is said in the first passage that they will hear the voice of the Son of God and live.

As far as regards the distinction into two classes, this doctrine agrees with that preached by St. Paul, where he affirms that his unbelieving countrymen "themselves allowed that there would be a resurrection of the dead, both of the just and the unjust (Acts 24:15). It may here be remarked that it is not necessary to infer from it being said in John v. 28-29, that "all that are in their graves shall hear his voice and come forth," that all will rise simultaneously. In Revelation 20:5, we have in clear terms, "This is the first resurrection." And again, in the next verse, "Blessed and holy is he that hath part in the first resurrection; on such the second death has no power." It is evident, therefore, that this is the resurrection of the just, and those who are thus "blessed and holy" are therefore exempt from mortality. This conclusion has very important bearing on our argument for immortality after the grave; for, on turning to v. 4 of the same chapter, we find that the partakers of this resurrection are described as the martyrs "who were beheaded for the witness of Jesus, and for the Word of God."

It seems, therefore, allowable to infer that this is the company of those who in Scripture are so often called the "elect," who by suffering, experience, and hope, are in this life "sealed" unto the day of redemption (Revelations 7: 2-8, and Ephesians 4:30). Also, we must realize that these chosen ones are said to have "lived and reigned with Christ a 'thousand years" (Rev. 20: 1-5). This period is also referred to as the Millennium, (described as the 'Peaceful Second Coming' later in the text). It is noted that the "rest of the dead lived not until the thousand years were finished." It is assumed that the interval of a thousand years existed between the just and the unjust.

It is also to be particularly noticed that the Revelator, speaking of what pertains to that interval of a thousand years says that he saw thrones and they sat upon them, and judgment was given to them (v.4). This is a very interesting passage that is not generally taught or studied by the church and needs exposure and close study. The reference here, is to the judgment undergone by those who have part in the first resurrection, because the rest of the dead do not rise to be judged until the thousand years are ended! As to the elect being judged, the teaching of Paul is very explicit, where he says, identifying himself with the company of the faithful, "We must all appear before the judgment-seat of Christ; that everyone may receive the things done through the body, according to what he hath done, whether good or bad" (2 Corinthians 5:10).

It must now be taken into account that the experience and the deeds of the present life alone determine whether any individual is or is not of the number of the elect. Those only who by the favor of God are justified in this life by works done through faith are reckoned among "the just" who partake of the first resurrection. But Scripture nowhere asserts that their spiritual state differs at their resurrection from what it was at the time of death; rather, it negates this assumption by describing their state in the interval as that of "sleep". Consequently, not being yet "made perfect," they have need to pass through the judgment just spoken of in order that by the completion of their spiritual creation they might be made ready for immortality. To them, it appears although there is punishment, there is no "condemnation," and, therefore, no "second death."

CHAPTER 9

SIGNS OF THE MILLENNIUM

Many Christians hold the view of the Second Coming as a time filled with calamity, fire and brimstone, punishment, and judgment. However, my focus is on making the connection between the third millennial thousand-year period and the reign of God's peace by Christ in its fullness, in the kingdom of God on earth. It is popularly called the Millennium. It is said to be, with some surprise, a part of the Second Coming. There has been much debate among theologians on eschatological (last days and end-time theories) predictions resulting from recent historical findings, such as the Dead Sea Scrolls, which came into light between 1947 and 1956. Many suspected historical biblical facts were substantiated by the findings.

We now live in a period two thousand years since the death and resurrection of Christ. The third Millennium is upon us. Several years prior to the event, there was an anticipation of major dysfunctions in technology and world communication systems. Concerns were centered around Y2K and the advent of the new Millennium. The changes expected to occur were to be both good and bad. Scripture clearly tells us that only God knows the day or the hour of this event. But as sincere worshipers, we look forward to the day when we will reign with Christ in the kingdom of God. We can never know exactly when, but we can be assured that these stages of the true Millennium will occur. It will be like no other event experienced in our history and will instate a new world without conflict, hate, or discord. The means by which this will be manifested are not yet known.

On July 23, 1995, a comet was discovered independently by two observers, Allan Hale and Thomas Bopp, both in the United States. Comet Hale-Bopp was considered to be one of the most fascinating discoveries during the twentieth century. It was visibly observed by scientists for eighteen months and said to be twice as long as the previous record holder, the Great Comet of 1811. It was a long way from the sun, and expectations were being raised that the comet would illuminate considerably by the time it moved near the earth. Even though it was difficult to predict its brilliance with any degree of accuracy, it was said that Hale-Bopp met or exceeded most predictions when it passed orbital expectations on April 1, 1997. It was then called the Great Comet of 1997.

Many envisioned this discovery as an omen for the coming of the new Millennium. Groups from all locations in the country met in designated places that were considered to be high-energy areas for celebration. Not knowing very much at the time about the relevance of the events, I encouraged my friends to come with me to a site in San Antonio where hundreds gathered to dance, celebrate, and bring in the dawning of a new age. I must say that it was a learning experience. Some Bible students made connections with prophecy Scriptures that made reference to the Second Coming found in Matthew 24:29–30, which speaks *to signs in the heavens,* saying, "The sun will be darkened, and the moon will not give its light; the stars will fall from heaven, and the powers of heaven will be shaken. Then the sign of the Son of Man will appear in heaven, and then all the tribes of the earth will mourn, and they will see the 'Son of Man coming on the clouds of heaven' with power and great glory'" (NRSV).

There is also a reference made to the signs in the heavens cited in a passage in Twyman's book, *The Emissary of Light: A Vision of Peace.*[12] Maria tells Twyman, "I am going to give you a sign that will put you at peace. In a very short time the whole world will see me flash through the sky with a tail of light. When you see this sign, know that the time is at hand when all things I spoke of will come to pass. For now, never forget your promise to me, and know that I will never forget you."

A week later Twyman was in Prescott, Arizona. As he was looking at the sky, he saw it—the comet. He said at first it didn't dawn on him that there was any particular significance to it, but then he remembered her words: "The whole world will see me flash through the sky with a tail of light. Then you'll know it has begun." The comet Hale-Bopp was more than an astronomical phenomenon to Twyman; it was thought to be a sign from heaven, a promise that everything was going according to plan. Some felt that because nothing major or earth shattering happened on the designated date, it was all a hoax. However, the date of the beginning could possibly be interpreted as the event in its infancy that continues to be in development until it reaches full maturity at the ordained time.

Because of the lengthy span of visibility and massive coverage in the media, Hale-Bopp was considered to be the most widely monitored comet in history, surpassing the impact made on the return of Halley's Comet in 1986. It was said that over 69 percent of Americans had viewed the comet by April 9, 1997. The comet was record-breaking, being the farthest comet from the sun ever observed by amateurs. Scientists recorded it as being brighter than magnitude zero for eight weeks, which is noted as being longer than any other recorded comet.

---

[12] James F. Twyman, *Emissary of Light: A Vision of Peace* (New York: Warner Books, 1996), 82.

There are many signs and omens identified with the Millennium. However, I am primarily concerned with immortality or near-death experiences. America is considered to be the most millenarian conscious of all nations by author Harold Bloom and most religious scholars. Our culture seems to be intrigued by angels, prophetic dreams, resurrection, and immortality. Many consider these preoccupations to be related to new age concepts, not realizing that their origins are found in ancient Hebraic, Sufi, and Christian traditions.

The link between immortality and the Millennium in my opinion is strongly related to the mystery of the Beloved Disciple John, which has been held in secrecy for the past two thousand years. The surfacing of this enigma at this particular time could be a sign in itself. As alluded to in the passage on John's mission (John 21), preparation of humanity for the Second Coming was part of his mission. The immortality Jesus gave him until his return was necessary for securing the peacemakers' victory over so-called sin and death. A group from the community of the Beloved Disciple, according to Twyman, evolved into beings of light over many years so a connection could be maintained between the physical and spiritual realms on earth.

John's work continues to be a work in progress so that fulfillment of the promises given to Adam and Eve in effect becomes a *covenant*. As James Challis concludes in his essay on immortality:

> God on His part promises happiness and immortality, but to be received only on stated conditions (See Gen. 3:15) wherein two parties are concerned: God on His part promises happiness and immortality, but to be received only on the conditions (Gen. 3:16-19) that labor and sorrow, pain and death, were ordained to be his lot, in order that he may be suitable to partake of the promise; and man's part was to submit to the

conditions, as being ordered by a "faithful Creator," and to look in faith for the fulfillment of the promise.

This same covenant might with more exactness be called a will or testament. And because the covenanted promise runs through the whole of Scriptures, it has been appropriately named the Scriptures of the Old Testament and of the New Testament which reveals an earlier stage of development of the same covenant.

A deeper understanding of the testaments can be seen in the Sacrament of the Lord's Super. It is justly regarded as the central ordinance of the Christian religion, and therefore, of necessity has relation to the means whereby immortality is secured.

Information revealed to James Twyman during his encounter with the Emissaries of Light indicated that the ongoing work of John the Beloved involves, primarily, preparing the peacemakers of God to take on a higher stage of spiritual development. As this light is activated within their hearts, others will recognize and activate this transforming power, which is already latent within their own hearts. The lyrics, "Let there be peace on earth, and let it begin with me" is a perfect example of how this process works.

Again, it is uniformly affirmed in Scripture that everyone will be judged "according to his works." Of course, words are included in works, for our Lord said expressly, "Every idle word that men shall speak, they shall give account thereof in the day of judgement; for by thy words thou shall be justified, and by thy words thou shall be condemned" (Matt. 12:36–37 NRSV). It would seem that the judgment, as being conducted by external means, takes account of human thoughts only so far as their consequences are manifested by overt deeds and spoken words. It is not the less true, according to the doctrine of the Lord himself in Mark 4:22 and Luke 7:17 (NRSV), that in the day of judgment, all secret hidden things will be revealed. The words in St. Mark, "Neither was anything kept secret but in order that it should come abroad," seem expressly to indicate the relation in which things hidden in the present age stand to the revelations of that day. St. Paul also writes to the Romans, speaking of them who have not received the law by direct communication:

> They show the work of the law written in their hearts, their conscience bearing them witness, and their thoughts, one with another, accusing, or also excusing, in the day when God shall judge the secrets of men, according to my gospel, through Jesus Christ. (Rom. 2:15–16 NRSV)

In *Omens of Millennium: The Gnosis of Angels, Dreams, and Resurrection*,[13] Harold Bloom states that one of the many unhappy oddities of contemporary United States is that so many of us are Bible-based yet have never read the Bible. He feels that this has much to do with the phenomenon of fundamentalism, which insists that the Bible is inerrant and for the most part declining the difficult labor of interpreting and reading its text. It is mentioned in his book that pollsters estimate that there are 10 million premillennialists among us—that is, people who expect Jesus to return, in his resurrected body, before he then inaugurates a thousand-year kingdom on earth, over which he will rule. Yet the premillennialists are only a small fraction of believers. He further states that more than 100 million American adults expect a Second Coming of Jesus, even if they do not necessarily believe that he will found the kingdom of God

---

[13] Harold Bloom, *Omens of Millenniums: The Gnosis of Angels, Dreams, and Resurrection,* New York: Riverhead Books, 1996.

in this world. His book has been, to him, written in the ancient conviction that:

> What makes us free is the knowing that the spark that is the innermost self necessarily involves knowing the self's potential ... If we are fragments of what was once a Fullness, then we can know what once we were and what we might yet be again.

CHAPTER 10

THE BUILDING OF RELATIONSHIP THROUGH EXPERIENCING GOD

One day as I was traveling to a specific location to join my church group for a bus outing, I came to a dead end. I did not know which road to take right or left. I was lost. As I sat there trying to make sense of the directions, the Spirit spoke to me on an inner level and said, "Seek my face!" I heard it but could not figure out what that had to do with me needing directions to the church bus. I did not give it much attention because I was more concerned about being lost. Running late, I hurriedly picked a turn, traveled several miles, and ended up at the same dead end location I had just left…(which I felt was strange). This happened two more times. Out of desperation, I promised the Lord, that I would do as he had asked and 'seek his face'. When I drove off the third time, I ended up at the bus location just in time. There was no doubt in my mind that 'getting lost' was God's way of getting my attention.

Of course I was very disturbed that the Lord would order me to do such a thing. This may have been why I failed to take the request seriously at first. How could God ask me to do this? I was a baptized believer, a member of the church since I was age twelve, and had been serving as a church musician since age fifteen! Being thirty-five years of age, I was embarrassed and insulted. After dealing with my frustration, I calmly told the Lord, "But I already know you." Finally, after coming to my senses and realizing that God was 'all-knowing', I decided to do as he had asked.

My world as I once knew it changed. New insights, books, spiritual groups, movies, new people, and organizations filled my world which thrilled me to the core. God knew just how to push my buttons and give me new life. It was through one of these groups that I learned about the existence of other earthly planes. At that time, of course, I could not see how I would ever need or benefit from that knowledge or experience. However, it did help me to understand and be open to the circumstances surrounding the existence and work of the Beloved Disciple John without question later in my search.

One night as I was lying across my bed exhausted after attending an event, I began to drift off to sleep. Before I lost consciousness, my eyes focused on the entrance of my bathroom and held a steady gaze. Then I saw a tall figure dressed in a long sackcloth dress walk pass the entrance. I could only see the side and back part of the body. The hips seemed feminine and the waist seemed small. It got my attention fully as it passed the entrance. I became alert semi-consciously without fear. A few seconds later, the figure came back to the entrance into the doorway and walked toward my bed. It had on brown leather sandal shoes. The sackcloth garment came to the ankles. It walked to the end of my bed where my head was lying. It stood over me. I looked down on the floor and began observing the feet, moving on up slowly to the shoulders and then the neck. As I was about to look at the face, I lost consciousness. It seemed as if I had fainted our of fear! I never spoke to anyone of this vision for years. It was as if I was afraid to do so. I can now, after so many years, but not in any detail.

During my early ministry preparation, I was informed by my spiritual mentor that I would experience an 'exploding sensation in my chest' as physical evidence that I was on the path to ministry. Several weeks later as I was sitting at the piano during a church service, a bursting of energy seemed to expand in my chest which made me bend over on the bench for relief. I knew that this was the experience I had been told about. I had already had an epiphany earlier and experienced a force knocking me to the floor after I had finished with my prayer time. An audible voice spoke to me while I was lying on the floor in fear, and said, "Walk worthy of the vocation wherein you are called!" Not knowing the meaning of the message, I begged for time to find the message in Scripture. At the time it sounded like Scripture but I did not know where it was located. The voice said, "Ephesians 4: and 1!" It was then that I realized that I was communicating with an intelligent source. I knew that the Source was God. I crawled to the side of my bed and asked in humble surrender, "What do you want me to do?"

I knew without a shadow of a doubt that these supernatural experiences were in preparation for ministry. I was inspired and ready to go! My relationship with God began to grow and increase. I found myself feeling lonely whenever I was not in the presence of God during the day. It was a regular routine to awaken early enough in the mornings to spend time in prayer and meditation. I also started taking notes in a journal to keep record of insights and instructions given to me through the Spirit.

Knowing God through experiences creates a relationship that is vital and necessary. You become a joint-heir in the kingdom world. As a joint-heir, we are cemented together with the Father, Son, Holy Spirit, and others. We live in the conviction expressed by the apostle Paul in Romans 8:38 that "I am convinced that neither death, nor life, nor angels, nor rulers, nor anything else in all creation, will be able to separate us from the love of God in Christ Jesus our Lord.

CHAPTER 11

SUMMARY

Throughout my adult life, I have maintained what felt like a divine impetus to understand as much as I could concerning Jesus' statement on John's 'remaining' until his return. As I saw this same reference to someone 'not tasting death' in the synoptic Gospels in Matthew, Mark, and Luke, I was convinced that Jesus was intentionally giving vital information and hints concerning his second coming. I also felt that he was giving validity to the possibility of immortality for those who were worthy during his lifetime.

There seemed to be an attempt by Jesus the Christ to stretch the imagination and raise the consciousness of his followers and disciples to think outside of the proverbial 'box'. Even if we would consider the resurrection to be for all humankind, good and evil...so be it! It will be especially so for those who have been faithful to Christ and shown their love and devotion to the Savior by practicing good works. In fact, the resurrection of the dead will be a joyful and salvation event: The Lord Jesus, as the Lord of history, will return gloriously on the last day to save forever those who belong to him, by making them participate in his appearance and glory. For this reason, Christians are joyously awaiting the Second Coming of the Lord as the moment of total salvation of one's whole being, soul and body, and as the full and perfect fulfillment of their hope. This sense of joy, peace, and hope is expressed by the words: "And we will be with the Lord forever." For our consideration, let's expand our thinking of the resurrection.

Thus, it is said that the victory over death announced by the Christian faith is for the whole person: for the soul and for the body. It would be pointless, however, to ask: "With what kind of body will we rise again?" or: "What will the eternal life of the saved be like after the final resurrection in soul and body?" These are questions which, for us who are only able to think about the life of the body in terms of time and space and, above all, in terms of human functions, would remain wrapped up in a profound mystery: A mystery which we must respect as God's mystery, because Scripture does not tell us anything on this point, at least as far as we know or desire to inquire. Of course, there is a hint in written Scripture where there is mention about the transformation that takes place in a seed which, when it is planted, grows into a tree: Between the seed and the tree there is certainly an identity, but there is also an essential difference. Something similar happens to the human body in the "resurrection of the dead": 1Corinthians 15: 35-56 states that "What is sown as perishable is raised imperishable. Sown in humiliation, it is raised in glory; sown in weakness, it is raised in power; sown a physical body, it is raised a spiritual body."

A "spiritual" body means a body completely transformed by the power of the Holy Spirit; but for us the meaning of this remains mysterious and obscure. The resurrection body should not be understood in a materialistic or physical sense. Jesus said as much when he rejected the materialism of the people of his day and rebuked them for not knowing "either the Scripture or the power of God": He said, "The children of this world marry; but those who have been judged worthy of a place in the world, and of the resurrection from the dead, do not marry, for they are no longer subject to death.

They are like angels; they are children of God, because they share in the resurrection.

In any case, in the midst of so much obscurity and uncertainty we still have the absolute certainty that, in virtue of Christ's resurrection, we are destined to conquer death, and to live eternally with God, participating in infinite happiness. Strengthened by this faith and this hope, the Christian, even in the face of death which seems to be the victor in human history can throw down this challenge: "Death is swallowed up; victory is won! O Death, where is your sting?

Death is not the destiny of humankind! We have and can demonstrate with rational arguments and conviction that we are IMMORTAL IN SPIRIT for eternity.

Let bronze be brought from Egypt; let Ethiopia hasten to stretch out its hands to God. Sing to God, O Kingdoms of the earth; sing praises to the Lord, O rider in the heavens, the ancient heavens; listen, he sends out his voice, his mighty voice. Psalms 68: 31-32, NRSV

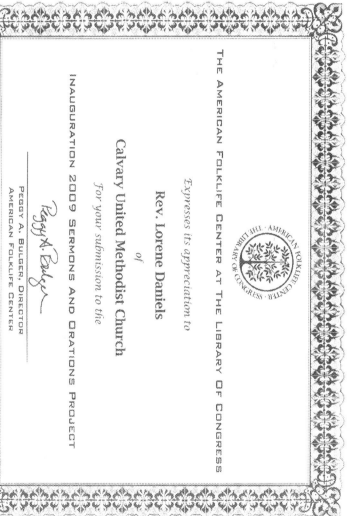

THE AMERICAN FOLKLIFE CENTER AT THE LIBRARY OF CONGRESS

Expresses its appreciation to

Rev. Lorene Daniels

of

Calvary United Methodist Church

For your submission to the

INAUGURATION 2009 SERMONS AND ORATIONS PROJECT

PEGGY A. BULGER, DIRECTOR
AMERICAN FOLKLIFE CENTER

Certificate of Appreciation from the Library of Congress

SELECTED BIBLIOGRAPHY

Bloom, Harold, *Omens of Millennium: The Gnosis of Angels, Dreams, and Resurrection* (New York: Riverhead, 1995)

Buchan, John, *Prester John*, (New York: George H. Doran Company, 1910)

Challis, James F, "An Essay on the Scriptural Doctrine of Immortality", http://Biblehub.com, June 5,1862.(web) (14 Nov.2014)

Chon, Norman, *Cosmos, Chaos, and the World to Come: The Ancient Roots of Apocalyptic Faith*, (New Haven and London: Yale University Press, 1993)

Koester, Craig R., *Symbolism in the fourth Gospel: Meaning, Mystery, Community* (Minneapolis: Fortress Press, 1995).

Quast, Kevin, *Peter and the Beloved Disciple: Figures for a Community in Crisis* (Worcester: Billing and Sons Ltd. 1989)

Steiger, Brad, *In My Soul I am Free,* (Memlo Park: IWP, 1983)

Twyman, James F, *Emissary of Light: A Vision of Peace*, (New York): Warner Books Inc., 19980

The Secret of the Beloved Disciple (Scotland: Finhorn Press, 2004) 85-89

Printed in the United States
By Bookmasters